Contents

Introduction

If you are wild about learning and wild about animals – this book is for you!

It will take you on a wild adventure, where you will practise key fractions skills and explore the amazing world of animals along the way.

Each fractions topic is introduced in a clear and simple way with lots of interesting activities to complete so that you can practise what you have learned.

Alongside every fractions topic you will uncover fascinating facts about baby animals.

When you have completed each topic, record the animals that you have seen and the skills that you have learned in the explorer's logbook on pages 28–29.

Good luck, explorer!

Alan Dobbs

Halves of shapes

A **fraction** is part of a whole. Each part has the same amount: the parts are equal.

Half ($\frac{1}{2}$) is a fraction. Half means that there are 2 equal parts.

This shape has half ($\frac{1}{2}$) coloured. Both halves are equal. Half of the whole shape has been coloured.

We can divide each half into smaller pieces. In the shapes below, each half is divided into 3 smaller pieces.

1 half of each shape is shaded.

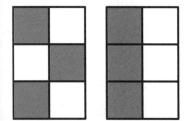

| Task 1 | Colour 1 half ($\frac{1}{2}$) of each shape. |

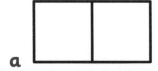

a

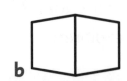

b

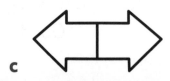

c

Task 2

Write $\frac{1}{2}$ under the shapes that have one half shaded.

a _____

b _____

c _____

d _____

Task 3

Shade each shape differently to show the fraction half ($\frac{1}{2}$).

a   b   c   d

WILD FACT

Meerkat pups are born in burrows. They crawl out after about 5 weeks. The other meerkats watch them carefully.

Now scamper over to pages 28–29 and fill in your explorer's logbook!

3

Finding half of a group

Each **half** of a group has the same (**equal**) amount.

Half of this group of 4 hoglets is 2!

FACT FILE

Animal:	Hedgehog
I live in:	Woodland, parks and gardens
I eat:	Mother's milk for the first 4 weeks, then worms and insects
My babies are called:	Hoglets

Task 1

How many hoglets are there in half of this group of 6?

_____

Task 2

Hoglets soon learn to find snails. How many snails would be left if a hoglet ate half of them?

_____ snails would be left.

WILD FACT

When hoglets are born their spines are soft and pink. They harden after a few days.

WILD FACT

Hoglets leave their mother when they are around 8 weeks old. They are able to take care of themselves and find their own food.

Task 3   Look at these groups. Find half of each one.

a Half of this group is _____

b Half of this group is _____

c Half of this group is _____

Now crawl over to pages 28–29 and fill in your explorer's logbook!

Quarters of shapes

When a shape or object is divided into **4 equal parts**, we say that it has been divided into **quarters**.

 This shape is divided into quarters. There are 4 equal parts. Each part is a quarter. There are 4 quarters in 1 whole. 1 quarter has been shaded.

If 2 quarters are shaded, the fraction looks like this. $\frac{2}{4}$

If 3 quarters are shaded, the fraction looks like this. $\frac{3}{4}$

Task 1   Shade one quarter ($\frac{1}{4}$) of each shape.
Shade a different quarter of each shape.

Task 2

Tick (✓) the shapes that have $\frac{1}{4}$ coloured.

a

b

c

d

Task 3

Write the shaded fraction for each shape.

a _____

b _____

c _____

Now sniff your way over to pages 28–29 and fill in your explorer's logbook!

Finding quarters of a group

When a group is split into quarters, each quarter is **equal**.

The whole splits into 4 groups that have the same amount.

This group of 8 bananas has been split into quarters. 1 quarter ($\frac{1}{4}$) is 2 bananas!

Task 1   The gorillas find some mangos.

a How many mangos are in $\frac{1}{4}$ of this group?   _____

b How many mangos are there in $\frac{3}{4}$ of the group?   _____

Task 2   Count the leaves.

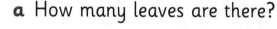

a How many leaves are there?   _____

b How many leaves are in $\frac{1}{4}$ of the total amount?   _____

c How many leaves are in $\frac{3}{4}$ of the total?   _____

Task 3

Look at these groups of rectangles. Each group has a fraction coloured. Match the coloured parts to their fraction names.

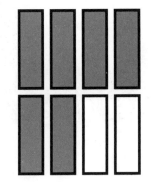

a

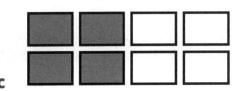

b

c

$\dfrac{1}{4}$

$\dfrac{2}{4}$

$\dfrac{3}{4}$

WILD FACT

Baby gorillas spend a lot of their time sleeping. The best place seems to be on top of mum!

Now swing over to pages 28–29 and fill in your explorer's logbook!

Thirds of shapes

A **third** is part of a shape, object or group that has been divided into **3 equal parts**.

 This shape is divided into thirds.

Three equal parts make up the whole.

Task 1   Colour 1 third ($\frac{1}{3}$) of each shape.

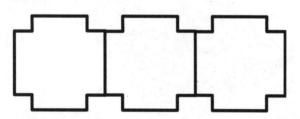 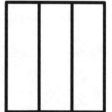 

Task 2   Tick (✓) the shapes that have $\frac{1}{3}$ coloured.

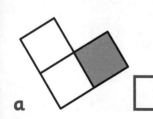

a ☐

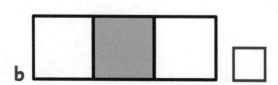

b ☐

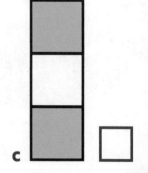

c ☐

Task 3

Kids are often fed bottles of milk by humans. A kid drinks 3 bottles of milk each day. Colour a third ($\frac{1}{3}$) of this group of bottles.

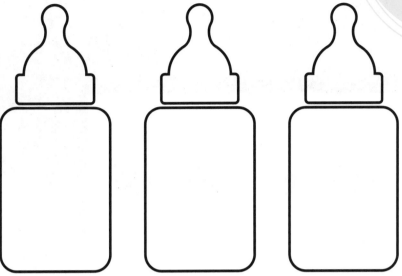

Now hop, skip and jump to pages 28–29 and fill in your explorer's logbook!

Finding thirds of a group

Here are 6 goslings.

A third ($\frac{1}{3}$) of the group is 2 goslings.

If we divide the group into thirds, there are 3 equal groups of 2 goslings.

WILD FACT

Geese are very protective of their babies. They will drive away anything that gets too close, even you!

FACT FILE

Animal: Goose

I live in: Wet places, such as lakes and reservoirs, and in farm ponds

I eat: Grass, insects, worms and shrimps

My babies are called: Goslings

Task 1

How many goslings are in a third ($\frac{1}{3}$) of this group?

_____

Task 2

There are 9 clumps of tasty grass in the field. The farmer has 3 goslings who love to eat grass. They each eat a third of the clumps.

a How many clumps of grass does each gosling eat? _____

b Write this as a fraction. _____

Task 3

Count this clutch of goose eggs.

a There are _____ eggs in the whole group.

b Divide the eggs into three equal groups to find how many eggs are in $\frac{1}{3}$ of the group.

$\frac{1}{3}$ is _____ eggs.

c Write this fraction in words. _____

Now paddle over to pages 28–29 and fill in your explorer's logbook!

Fractions of measurements

In fractions of a measurement, each part is an equal amount. This measurement is 12 cm.

0 1 2 3 4 5 6 7 8 9 10 11 12
CM

Half ($\frac{1}{2}$) of this measurement is 6 cm.

Each half is the same size.

0 1 2 3 4 5 6
CM

A quarter ($\frac{1}{4}$) is 3 cm.
A third ($\frac{1}{3}$) is 4 cm.

0 1 2 3
CM

0 1 2 3 4
CM

Task 1 Look at the rulers. What would be $\frac{1}{2}$ of each measurement?

0 1 2 3 4 5 6 7 8 9 10
CM

a _____ cm

0 1 2 3 4 5 6 7 8 9 10 11 12 13 14 15 16
CM

b _____ cm

0 1 2 3 4 5 6 7 8 9 10 11 12 13 14 15 16 17 18 19 20
CM

c _____ cm

Task 2

Look at these turtle hatchlings. Each one is a different length.

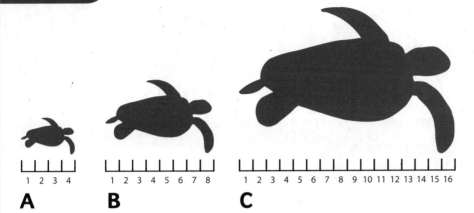

A   B   C

What would a quarter ($\frac{1}{4}$) of each measurement be?

a Turtle A (4 cm)   _____ cm

b Turtle B (8 cm)   _____ cm

c Turtle C (16 cm)   _____ cm

Turtles spend all their lives in the sea. They only come to land to lay their eggs on the beach.

Task 3

Look at these rulers. What is $\frac{1}{3}$ of each total measurement?

(Remember that each third is one of 3 equal parts of the whole.)

a _____ cm

b _____ cm

Newly hatched turtles dig their way out of the sand and head straight for the sea!

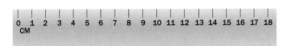

c _____ cm

Now swim over to pages 28–29 and fill in your explorer's logbook!

More fractions of measurements

Mass is a measurement of how heavy something is. To find a fraction of a mass, you have to divide it into equal amounts.

Here is an example.

The mass of this lion cub is 4 kg. Each **half** ($\frac{1}{2}$) of this amount is 2 kg.

When the two masses are added together, you have the whole mass of 4 kg.
A **quarter** ($\frac{1}{4}$) of this mass is 1 kg. Each measurement of weight is **equal**.

1 kg + 1 kg + 1 kg + 1 kg = 4 kg

Each equal part is 1 **quarter** ($\frac{1}{4}$) of the whole amount.

Task 1 What is **half** ($\frac{1}{2}$) the mass of each lion cub?

a The mass of **Cub A** is 6 kg

Half = _____ kg

b The mass of **Cub B** is 8 kg

Half = _____ kg

c The mass of **Cub C** is 16 kg

Half = _____ kg

FACT FILE

Animal: Lion
I live in: Grasslands and savannas
I eat: Mother's milk for the first 6 months, then meat my mother catches for me
My babies are called: Cubs

Task 2

Capacity is measured in **litres** (l). Finding a fraction of capacity is the same as finding a fraction of other measurements. Remember, each part has to be an equal amount!

Lion cubs drink a lot of milk! Each bottle holds 1 litre of milk.

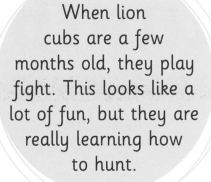

WILD FACT

When lion cubs are a few months old, they play fight. This looks like a lot of fun, but they are really learning how to hunt.

a One cub drank this many litres of milk:

How many litres did the cub drink? _____ litres

b Another cub drank half ($\frac{1}{2}$) this amount. How many litres did this cub drink? _____ litres

c A third cub drank 3 quarters ($\frac{3}{4}$) of the amount that the first cub drank. How many litres did this cub drink?_____ litres

WILD FACT

Lion cubs are born blind. They only open their eyes when they are 6 weeks old, then they are quick to explore!

Task 3 Count the bottles of milk.

a How many litres are there in total? _____ litres

b What is $\frac{1}{4}$ of this amount? _____ litres

c What is 1 third ($\frac{1}{3}$) of the total? _____ litres

Now play fight over to pages 28–29 and fill in your explorer's logbook!

Fractions of numbers

WILD FACT

When they are just a few weeks old, calves enjoy playing with each other. What they are really doing is sorting out how important they are in the herd!

Finding a **fraction** of a number is like finding a fraction of a measurement.

$\frac{1}{4}$ of 4 = 1 (1 + 1 + 1 + 1 = 4)

$\frac{1}{2}$ of 4 = 2 (2 + 2 = 4)

$\frac{1}{3}$ of 6 = 2 (2 + 2 + 2 = 6)

Each part has to be **equal** to be a **fraction**.

FACT FILE

Animal:	Cow
I live in:	Grasslands and also on farms
I eat:	Mother's milk for the first 9 months, then grass
My babies are called:	Calves

Task 1

Here are 20 calves.

a What is half of 20? _____

b Write this as a repeated addition. ____ + ____ = 20

c What is a quarter of 20? _____

d Write this number as a repeated addition.

____ + ____ + ____ + ____ = 20

Task 2 Use a separate sheet to work out the answers to these questions. Then write your answers below.

a There are 6 calves in a field. How many calves are $\frac{1}{3}$ of 6?

_____ calves

b In another field, there are 9 calves. What is $\frac{1}{3}$ of 9?

_____ calves

c In the biggest field, there are 21 calves. What is $\frac{1}{3}$ of this herd of calves? $\frac{1}{3}$ of 21 = _____ calves

WILD FACT

Within minutes of being born, a calf can stand up. Shortly after that, it can run around with its mother.

Task 3 Use a separate sheet to work out the answers to these questions. Then write your answers below.

a What is $\frac{1}{4}$ of 16? _____

b What is $\frac{1}{2}$ of 16? _____

c What is $\frac{3}{4}$ of 16? _____

d 10 is half of what number? _____

e 10 is $\frac{1}{3}$ of what number? _____

f 10 is $\frac{1}{4}$ of what number? _____

Now run over to pages 28–29 and fill in your explorer's logbook!

Equivalent fractions

Equivalent fractions have the same value.

This square has been divided into 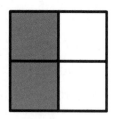 quarters ($\frac{1}{4}$). There are 4 equal parts. Two quarters ($\frac{2}{4}$) have been coloured. $\frac{2}{4} = \frac{1}{2}$ of the square.

2 quarters are equivalent (equal) to 1 half.

WILD FACT

Tadpoles develop quickly. They grow their back legs first and then their front legs. Finally, they can crawl out of the water. They still have a tail, but now they are known as froglets.

Task 1

Answer these equivalent fraction questions. An example has been done for you.

$$\frac{1}{4} \quad + \quad \frac{1}{4} \quad = \quad \frac{1}{2}$$

a $\frac{1}{4} + \frac{1}{4} + \frac{1}{4} + \frac{1}{4} =$ _____ halves

b $\frac{1}{4} + \frac{1}{4} + \frac{1}{4} + \frac{1}{4} + \frac{1}{4} + \frac{1}{4} =$ _____ halves

c $\frac{1}{4} + \frac{1}{4} + \frac{1}{4} + \frac{1}{4} + \frac{1}{4} + \frac{1}{4} + \frac{1}{4} + \frac{1}{4} + \frac{1}{4} + \frac{1}{4} =$ _____ halves

Task 2
We know that 4 quarters = 2 halves and that 2 halves = 1 whole.

a How many quarters are there in 2 wholes?   _____ quarters

b How many halves is this equivalent to?   _____ halves

c How many wholes do 6 halves equal?   _____ wholes

d How many quarters do 6 halves equal?   _____ quarters

Task 3
Complete the table to show the equivalent fractions and wholes.

Quarters	Halves	Wholes
4		1
		4
	10	

WILD FACT

As soon as tadpoles hatch, they eat the clear jelly that protected them as they grew.

Now wriggle over to pages 28–29 and fill in your explorer's logbook!

Wholes and fractions

When fractions add up to more than a whole, this is shown as a whole and a fraction. Look at these shapes.

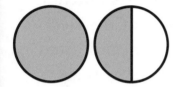

1 whole $\frac{1}{2}$ **We write this as** $1\frac{1}{2}$

Fractions can also be added even when they are different. For example, 2 halves and 1 quarter equal $1\frac{1}{4}$.

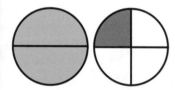

2 halves $\frac{1}{4}$ **We write this as** $1\frac{1}{4}$

WILD FACT

A joey is tiny when it is first born, but it grows really fast in its mother's pouch.

Task 1　Write the wholes and fractions.

a 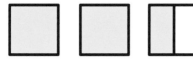 = _____

b 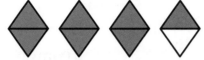 = _____

c  = _____

Task 2　Add these fractions. An example has been done for you.

$$\frac{1}{2} + \frac{1}{2} + \frac{1}{2} + \frac{1}{2} + \frac{1}{2} = 2\frac{1}{2}$$

a $\frac{1}{4} + \frac{1}{4} + \frac{1}{4} + \frac{1}{4} + \frac{1}{4}$ = _____

b $\frac{1}{2} + \frac{1}{2} + \frac{1}{2} + \frac{1}{2} + \frac{1}{2} + \frac{1}{2} + \frac{1}{2} + \frac{1}{2} + \frac{1}{2}$ = _____

c $\frac{1}{3} + \frac{1}{3} + \frac{1}{3} + \frac{1}{3}$ = _____

Task 3　Add these fractions. An example has been done for you.

$$\frac{1}{2} + \frac{1}{2} + \frac{1}{4} + \frac{1}{4} + \frac{1}{4} = 1\frac{3}{4}$$

a $\frac{1}{4} + \frac{1}{4} + \frac{1}{4} + \frac{1}{4} + \frac{1}{2}$ = _____

b 1 whole + $\frac{1}{2} + \frac{1}{2} + \frac{1}{4}$ = _____

c 2 wholes + $\frac{1}{2} + \frac{1}{2} + \frac{1}{4}$ = _____

WILD FACT

Joeys travel in their mother's pouch until they are almost 2 years old.

Now bounce to pages 28–29 and fill in your explorer's logbook!

Counting in fractions

You use the same rule for counting in fractions as you do for counting whole numbers. They should be in order – either getting bigger or getting smaller.

If we count in halves, the order looks like this:

$\frac{1}{2}$	1	$1\frac{1}{2}$	2	$2\frac{1}{2}$	3	$3\frac{1}{2}$	4	$4\frac{1}{2}$	5

Task 1 Count to five using halves and fill in the boxes. The first part has been done for you.

$\frac{1}{2}$	1	$1\frac{1}{2}$	2	$2\frac{1}{2}$				

WILD FACT

Otter pups can spend a long time in the water. Their thick, waterproof coat protects them.

Task 2

Now count in quarters to 3 and fill in the boxes. The first part has been done for you.

$\frac{1}{4}$	$\frac{1}{2}$	$\frac{3}{4}$	1								

Task 3

Put these wholes and fractions into the grid in order from smallest to biggest.

1	$\frac{3}{4}$	$5\frac{1}{2}$	$\frac{1}{4}$	$2\frac{3}{4}$	$\frac{1}{2}$	$3\frac{3}{4}$	$1\frac{1}{2}$	$1\frac{3}{4}$

Smallest   Biggest

WILD FACT

Otters are born with webbed feet, but they won't use them for swimming for a few months.

Now swim over to pages 28–29 and fill in your explorer's logbook!

Quick test

Now try these questions. Give yourself 1 mark for every correct answer – but only if you answer each part of the question correctly.

1 **Shade half ($\frac{1}{2}$) of each shape.**

2 **Tick (✓) the shape that has $\frac{1}{4}$ shaded.**

3 **What fraction of this shape is shaded?**

_____

4 **Circle $\frac{1}{4}$ of this group of goose eggs.**

5 **Shade $\frac{1}{3}$ of this shape.**

6 **4 goat kids weigh 20 kg altogether. How much does one kid weigh?** _____

26

7 Shade $\frac{3}{4}$ of this shape.

8 4 calves share this amount of grass equally. How many clumps of grass does 1 calf eat?

_____

9 How many is half ($\frac{1}{2}$) of this group of cubs?

_____

10 Circle three-quarters ($\frac{3}{4}$) of this group of milk bottles.

11 Look at these fractions. What is their total in wholes and fractions?

$\frac{1}{2}$ $\frac{1}{2}$ $\frac{1}{4}$ $\frac{1}{4}$ _____

12 This number line starts at $2\frac{1}{2}$. Counting up in halves, fill in the empty places.

$2\frac{1}{2}$

How did you do? 1–3 Try again! 4–6 Good try!
7–9 Great work! 10–12 Excellent exploring!

/12

27

Explorer's Logbook

Tick off the topics as you complete them and then colour in the star.

Halves of shapes ☐

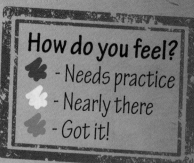

Finding half of a group ☐

Quarters of shapes ☐

Finding quarters of a group ☐

Thirds of shapes ☐

Finding thirds of a group ☐

Fractions of measurements ☐

More fractions of measurements ☐

Fractions of numbers ☐

Equivalent fractions ☐

Wholes and fractions ☐

Counting in fractions ☐

Answers

Pages 2–3

Task 1

a   **b**   **c**

(either half shaded)

Task 2

b and **d**

Task 3

Any 3 sections of each shape shaded

Pages 4–5

Task 1

3

Task 2

5

Task 3

a 6 **b** 10 **c** 9

Pages 6–7

Task 1

1 section shaded in each shape; each shape shows a different section shaded

Task 2

a and **d** ticked

Task 3

a $\frac{2}{4}$ **b** $\frac{1}{4}$ **c** $\frac{3}{4}$

Pages 8–9

Task 1

a 1 **b** 3

Task 2

a 12 **b** 3 **c** 9

Task 3

a $\frac{3}{4}$ **b** $\frac{1}{4}$ **c** $\frac{2}{4}$

Pages 10–11

Task 1

Any one section shaded in each shape.

Task 2

 ✓ 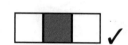 ✓

Task 3

1 bottle shaded

Pages 12–13

Task 1

2

Task 2

a 3 **b** $\frac{1}{3}$

Task 3

a 18

b 6

c one-third or a third

Pages 14–15

Task 1

a 5 cm **b** 8 cm **c** 10 cm

Task 2

a 1 cm **b** 2 cm **c** 4 cm

Task 3

a 3 cm **b** 4 cm **c** 6 cm

Pages 16–17

Task 1

a 3 kg **b** 4 kg **c** 8 kg

Task 2

a 8 litres **b** 4 litres **c** 6 litres

Task 3

a 12 litres **b** 3 litres **c** 4 litres

Pages 18–19

Task 1

a 10 **b** 10 + 10 = 20

c 5 **d** 5 + 5 + 5 + 5 = 20

Task 2

a 2 **b** 3 **c** 7

Task 3

a 4
b 8
c 12
d 20
e 30
ƒ 40

Pages 20–21

Task 1

a 2 halves
b 3 halves
c 5 halves

Task 2

a 8 quarters
b 4 halves
c 3 wholes
d 12 quarters

Task 3

Quarters	Halves	Wholes
4	2	1
16	8	4
20	10	5

Pages 22–23

Task 1

a $2\frac{1}{2}$ **b** $3\frac{1}{2}$ **c** $4\frac{1}{2}$

Task 2

a $1\frac{1}{4}$ **b** $4\frac{1}{2}$ **c** $1\frac{1}{3}$

Task 3

a $1\frac{1}{2}$ **b** $2\frac{1}{4}$ **c** $3\frac{1}{4}$

Pages 24–25

Task 1

$\frac{1}{2}$	1	$1\frac{1}{2}$	2	$2\frac{1}{2}$
3	$3\frac{1}{2}$	4	$4\frac{1}{2}$	5

Task 2

$\frac{1}{4}$	$\frac{1}{2}$	$\frac{3}{4}$	1	$1\frac{1}{4}$	$1\frac{1}{2}$
$1\frac{3}{4}$	2	$2\frac{1}{4}$	$2\frac{1}{2}$	$2\frac{3}{4}$	3

Task 3

$\frac{1}{4}$	$\frac{1}{2}$	$\frac{3}{4}$	1	$1\frac{1}{2}$
$1\frac{3}{4}$	$2\frac{3}{4}$	$3\frac{3}{4}$	$5\frac{1}{2}$	

Pages 26–27

1 1 section of each shape shaded

2 ✓

3 $\frac{3}{4}$

4 2 eggs circled
5 1 section shaded
6 5 kg
7 Any 9 sections shaded
8 2
9 4
10 9 bottles circled
11 $1\frac{1}{2}$

12 $2\frac{1}{2}$ 3 $3\frac{1}{2}$ 4 $4\frac{1}{2}$ 5 $5\frac{1}{2}$ 6 $6\frac{1}{2}$ 7

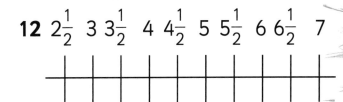

Well done, explorer!

You have finished your fractions adventure!

Explorer's pass

Name: _____

Age: _____

Date: _____

Draw a picture of yourself in the box!